D1715612

What I Love About You

What I Love About You

Copyright © 2009 Hallmark Licensing, LLC

Published by Hallmark Books,
a division of Hallmark Cards, Inc.,
Kansas City, MO 64141
Visit us on the Web at Hallmark.com.

Writer and Editor: Megan Langford
Art Director: Kevin Swanson
Designer: Mary Eakin
Production Artist: Dan Horton

ISBN: 978-1-59530-258-8
BOK1144

Printed and bound in China
JUL14

To one of my very **favorite** people,

_____,

Do you know how much I love you?
(Hint: It's a whole lot.) I don't want to get all
mushy gushy, but I hope you always remember
that I think you're pretty darn special.

Love,

_____

Three words that best describe you are:

_____

_____

_____

My favorite thing to do with you is:

_____

_____

_____

My favorite nickname for you is:

_____

_____

_____

If you were a **cookie**, you'd be:

☐ chocolate chip
(loved by everybody)

☐ gingersnap
(a little zippy)

☐ peanut butter
(always classic)

☐ triple chocolate chunk
(fun and funky)

The first time I saw you, I felt:

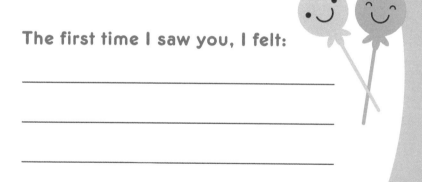

_____

_____

_____

I'm so **proud** of you because:

_____

_____

_____

If you were a movie, you'd be:

☐ a slapstick comedy

☐ a serious drama

☐ an action-adventure film

☐ a melodramatic musical

☐ an animated movie

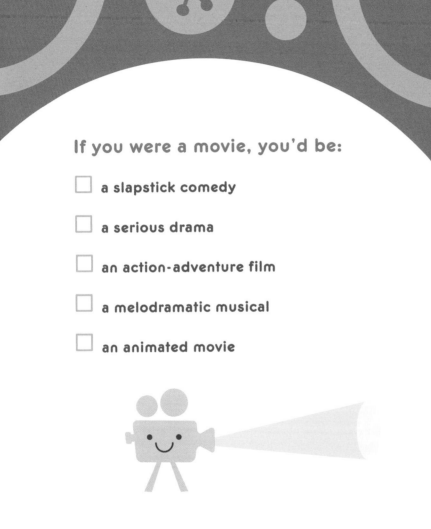

A story about you that I never get tired of telling is:

_____

_____

_____

Thank you for teaching me how to:

_____

_____

_____

I love it when you help me:

_____

_____

_____

I love it when you:

- ☐ sing
- ☐ play sports
- ☐ skip
- ☐ play video games
- ☐ act silly
- ☐ laugh
- ☐ do the chicken dance
- ☐ run

- ☐ tell jokes
- ☐ draw
- ☐ make funny faces
- ☐ read
- ☐ do your homework
- ☐ _____
- ☐ _____

When I brag about you, this is what I tell people:

_____

_____

_____

laugh

You always make me laugh when you:

_____

_____

_____

If you were peanut butter, you'd be:

☐ creamy

☐ crunchy

☐ the kind with the jelly mixed in

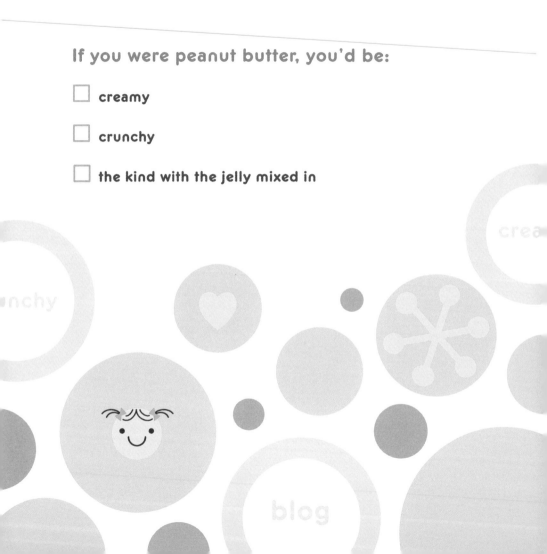

If I wrote a blog about you, I'd call it:

_____

_____

_____

Here are some ways you've changed my life:

_____

_____

_____

**If I wrote a book about you,
the title would be:**

_____

_____

_____

You are:

- [ ] fun
- [ ] caring
- [ ] kind
- [ ] loving
- [ ] hardworking
- [ ] considerate
- [ ] brave
- [ ] happy
- [ ] funny
- [ ] silly
- [ ] creative
- [ ] strong
- [ ] beautiful
- [ ] independent
- [ ] awesome
- [ ] _____
- [ ] _____

I always appreciate it when you:

_____

_____

_____

The thing I admire most about you is:

_____

_____

_____

If you were an animal, you'd be:

☐ a dog (friendly and ready to play)

☐ a swan (graceful and elegant)

☐ a cat (quiet and observant)

☐ a bird (ready to spread your wings and fly)

☐ a giraffe (always reaching for the stars)

☐ _____

The quirky things I love about you are:

_____

_____

_____

I can't believe how time has flown by . . .

It's only _____ years and _____ months
until you get your driver's license!

It's only _____ years and _____ months
until you graduate from high school!

It's only _____ years and _____ months
until you're old enough to vote!

I predict that when you grow up,
you'll be:

_____

_____

_____

If _____ was an Olympic
sport, you'd win the gold medal for sure!

amazing

You are:

☐ fantastic

☐ superb

☐ amazing

☐ wonderful

☐ all of the above

I'll never forget the first time you:

_____

_____

_____

If you were a superhero, you'd be:

_____

_____

_____

If you were in a rock band, it would be called:

_____

_____

_____

In your band, you would be:

☐ the lead singer

☐ the guitarist

☐ the bass player

☐ the drummer

☐ the kazoo player

I love the little everyday things
we do, like:

_____

_____

_____

I can't help smiling every time you:

_____

_____

_____

As you grow up, my advice to you is:

_____

_____

_____

**Look! Here are the two of us.
(Aren't we adorable?)**

(add photo here)

If you enjoyed this book,
would you let us know?

☐ yes

☐ no

☐ maybe later

Hallmark would
love to hear from you!
Please send your
comments to:

Hallmark Book Feedback
P.O. Box 419034
Mail Drop 215
Kansas City, MO 64141

Or e-mail us at:
booknotes@hallmark.com